The World's Best Yiddish Dirty Jokes

With warmest wishes,
M. "P."

The World's Best Yiddish Dirty Jokes

Mr."P"

With drawings by Robbie Stillerman

Citadel Press / Secaucus, N.J.

© 1984 by Citadel Press

All rights reserved
Published by Citadel Press
A division of Lyle Stuart Inc.
120 Enterprise Ave., Secaucus, N.J. 07094

In Canada: Musson Book Company
A division of General Publishing Co. Limited
Don Mills, Ontario

Manufactured in the United States of America

ISBN 0-8065-0887-7

The
World's Best
Yiddish Dirty
Jokes

I t is the period about 1910, the Lower East Side. The "greener"—the greenhorn cousin—has just arrived from Europe. He is unable to speak English, he does not have a trade. So, what is there to do? He must learn to provide for himself. The family helps him go into business. He rents a pushcart, the family lends him the money to stock it with goods, and he fills it up with pants (hayzen) and socks (zocken). And so he goes forth, pushing his pushcart along the streets and avenues as he shouts his wares, "Hayzen, zocken...hayzen, zocken."

Although business has been weak, he persists. On the fourth day, as he is pushing along, shouting, "Hayzen, zocken," a lady on the third floor of a tenement motions to him to come up.

Once in the apartment she says that she has observed him for the last three days, that she likes the way he looks, he appeals to her, that she is a widow and hasn't been with a man in some time, that she would be truly grateful if he would go to bed with her.

After they make love and he is about to leave, she presses a ten dollar bill into his hand and thanks him.

Ten dollars! That's more than he probably would earn all week. So he is inspired, and with vigor continues his route shouting, "Hayzen, zocken, fockin...hayzen, zocken, fockin."

Jake and Becky were celebrating their 50th wedding anniversary.

They returned to the same hotel, the same room where they spent their honeymoon night.

The time is 2:00 a.m. Jake nudges Becky in bed and says, "Becky—derlang mir die tzeyner, ich vill dir a beis geben."

TRANSLATION: "Hand me my teeth, so I can nibble on you."

3

It is Sunday afternoon. Mr and Mrs. Schwartz's daughter, Feyge, has brought a young man, Mendel, home to introduce to them. However, during the afternoon the parents notice that Mendel visits the bathroom about every half hour.

Says Mr. Schwartz to Mrs. Schwartz, "Gay, zeh vos is der mehr mit ihm. Es ken zein az er is a kranker."

So Mrs. Schwartz follows the young man and asks him if he is having a problem, she has noticed he makes frequent trips to the bathroom.

The young man explains that he is well, he is not sick. But he is so overcome by his feelings for their daughter that periodically he must relieve himself in the bathroom.

So Mrs. Schwartz returns and Mr. Schwartz asks, "Vos far a krenk is mit ihm?" Mrs Schwartz replies, "A zah krenk af dir."

TRANSLATION: "Gay, zeh...." = "Go see what is the matter with him. Maybe he's a sick person."

"Vos far..." = "What kind of sickness does he have?"

"A zah..." = "You should have such a sickness."

The schnorrer comes to call on the town's wealthiest Jew. But to no avail. He is rebuffed. He tries the front gate and it is locked. He tries the back gate and it is locked. So he bellows out, "Der ballobos vos vaynt doh vet nit leben mehr vie drei teg."

The owner runs out frightened and asks why did the schnorrer say what he did.

To which the schnorrer answered, "Ven es is vershpart fuhn forent und fuhn hinten ken men nit leben mehr vie drei teg."

TRANSLATION: "Der ballobos..." = "The owner of this house will not live more than three days."
"Ven es is..." = "When one is plugged up from the front and from the back one can only live three days."

The schadchen had brought a young man to meet Becky. The young man was interested in marrying an eydele meydel and was much dismayed when Becky interrupted their conversation by jumping out of her chair and announcing, "Az ich darf gehn pishen."

Later the schadchen told her that she must be more refined, that if she had a "nature call" she should say something like, "Anshuldig, ich darf gehn benetzen die blummen."

And so the next time the schadchen brought a young man to meet Becky, she excused herself by saying, "Anshuldig, ich darf gehn benetzen die blummen und kacken echet."

TRANSLATION: "Az ich..." = "I have to go piss."
                        "Anshuldig..." = Pardon, I have to go water the flowers."
                        "Und kacken..." = "And shit, too."

In the shtetl, the townspeople were offended. It was degrading to have a Jewish prostitute. The committee agreed it was the responsibility of the rabbi to communicate the community's feelings to the kurveh, to either stop or leave the village.

The rabbi agrees, he goes after lunch and four hours later the shamus goes to fetch him. The rabbi is just coming out of the door.

Shamus: "Rabbi, what happened? What took so long?"

Rabbi: "I don't know why everyone is complaining. She's such an interesting, nice lady. What do they want from her?"

Shamus: "Varshilivet dem kruhk, und mir vellen gehn tzum davening."

TRANSLATION: "Button your fly, and we'll go to the prayers."

Becky is spending her honeymoon night at her mother's home. About 2:00 in the morning her mother is awakened by screaming.

Becky is running up and down the hall. She is very upset.

Mother: "Becky, vos is? Bist du mishuga?"

Becky: "Oh Momma, ich bin nit mishuga, er is mishuga, er knicht aff menschen."

TRANSLATION: "Becky, vos..." = "Becky, what is it? Are you crazy?"

"Oh Momma, ich..." = "Oh Momma, I am not crazy, he is crazy, he climbs all over people."

Picture the Lower East Side, about 1910 at the Second Avenue Theater. It is the home of heightened stark realism.

The house lights dim, the stage lights up. The setting is a woman's bedroom. A young lady enters, goes behind a folding screen where she begins to undress and change into her nightgown. She proceeds to the wash basin where she washes her hands and face and brushes her teeth. Then she proceeds to the vanity where she brushes her hair.

Then, she climbs into bed and as she is about to shut off the lights a voice from the second balcony booms, "Vos is? Du darfs sich nit ois pischen?"

TRANSLATION: "Whats the matter? Don't you have to take a leak?"

The gabeh was seen by fellow congregants at the local brothel.

Congregant: "Vos tust du daw? Es past nit."
Gabeh: "Vos sohl schotten? Men darf doh nit essen."

TRANSLATION: "Vos tust..." = "What are you doing here? It's unsuitable."

"Vos sohl..." = "What harm can it do? I don't have to eat here."

A man and woman became acquainted at a Miami hotel. Before they know it, they are eating together, drinking together, and finally going to bed together, making love.

Later, she begins to cry.

He: "Why are you crying?"

She: "This should never have happened to me. I am married. My husband is a furrier, he works so hard, and he is taking care of the children and our beautiful home. He said I should go to Florida for two weeks, that it would do me a lot of good."

He comforted her, they had another drink, made love and he began to cry.

She: "Why are you crying?"

He: "I'm married too. I'm a baker, I work very hard and my wife insisted that I should go to Miami for two weeks in the sun. She is such a good wife and mother. This should never have happened to me."

So, she comforted him and they started to make love again.

Un a gantzen nacht hoben sey getrent und geveynt, getrent un geveynt.

TRANSLATION: And all night long they screwed and cried, screwed and cried.

J ake and Sam had been partners in a shmata factory for years and they knew one another as you would know the five fingers of your own hand.

Sam finally took his first vacation in years to Florida, but couldn't resist calling Jake to see how things were.

"Oy, Sam, can you imagine, we had a burglary last night and they took all the money." And Sam said in a friendly but firm and suffering manner, "Jake, layg tzurick."

TRANSLATION: "Jake, put it back."

The rabbi had died but the rebetzen had decided that life must go on and she wanted to remarry. The town was small, so her selection was quite limited. The local balagolah won her hand. No doubt her social standing would probably fall, but she was a realist.

It was on the honeymoon when the new husband approached her with, "Nu, Becky, vie is heint babacht?" She told him no. The rabbi used to tell her that it was an avera to make love on Lag Baomer. He countered that his niece married the son of a great scholar, the head of a Yeshiva, and he always said that it was a mitzvah to make love on this night.

On the second night, he invited her again and she offered another objection from the rabbi. But, again he produced evidence of a more learned scholar to whom he was related that proved that she would be acquiring a mitzvot.

An so it went on for a full week.

When she finally returned to her hometown, the local women asked her about being married to the balagolah, to which she replied, "Nu, a zay shayn vie die rebbi is er nit... un a zay helig vie di rebbi is er nit... ober, er hut a zah teyere michpocha!"

TRANSLATION: "Nu, Becky, vie..." = "Well, Becky, how about getting together tonight?"
"Nu, a say..." = "Well, he's not as handsome as the rabbi... and he's not as holy as the rabbi... but he has the most wonderful relatives!"

The doctor is explaining the urinalysis to Yenta.

Doctor: "You have 2% sugar, 3% salt, 5% red corpuscles and 8% white corpuscles."

Yenta: "Und ich hab gedeynkt as es is alles pissheches."

TRANSLATION: "And I thought it was just piss."

Two gentlemen are enjoying their daily promenade, at which time they generally discuss the important world issues.

The first: "Du farstays Einstein's Theory of Relativity?"

The second: "Yeh."

The first: "Erkler mir, vos meynt es?"

The second: "Dos is a za zach, vu es is the zelba, ober fort nit the selbe."

The first: "Du kenst mir geben a beispiel?"

The second: "Nu, sog, as du shtelst arreyn dein tzung in mein toches, host due a tzung in toches und ich hub a tzung in toches. Kenst sehn as es is die zelba, ober es is fort nit the zelba."

TRANSLATION: The first: "Do you understand Einstein's...?"

The second: "Yes."

The first: "Tell me, what does it mean?"

The second: "It's like this. It's something that is the same but really not the same."

The first: "Can you give me an example?"

The second: "Say, for example, that you put your tongue in my ass. Then you have a tongue in the ass, and I have a tongue in the ass. You can see it's the same, but not the same."

18

Lapidus broke his engagement with Becky and sold the returned ring to Cohen the jeweler for $300.00. Lapidus returns to buy back the ring for $400.00. Next week, Cohen buys it back for $500.00. Lapidus buys it back again for $600.00.

One day Lapidus sells it to another customer for $1200.00. Cohen becomes irate and says, "Gaylim, farvus hust du es farkeyft zu ananderen? Mir hoben bayde gemacht a zah fineim leben fun der ring."

TRANSLATION: "You fool, why did you sell it to someone else? We were both making a good living from the ring."

It's a beautiful summer day.

Two young medical students are discussing their studies when they observe an elderly man walking in the most peculiar fashion. He is bent over, walking, leaning toward the left, dragging his right leg, the left hand cupping his crotch, and the right in his back pocket.

One student observes, "See that man, he is so bent over due to a condition of hardening of the arteries on the pelvis. He must be in such great pain."

The second observes, "I must disagree. It is a classic condition. The man has ulcers, and he is in the midst of an attack. That's why he's so bent over."

They finally approach the gentleman to confirm which diagnosis is right, and explain that they have observed him. They repeat their diagnoses and ask which of them is wrong.

He answers, "Ihr hut beyde gemacht a toves, und ich hub echecht gemacht a toves. Ich hob gevelt geben a fortz, hob is ungemacht in die hayzen."

TRANSLATION: "You two have made a mistake, and I also made a mistake. I wanted to fart, but I shit in my pants."

The town spinster had married, much to everyone's surprise, and when she returned from the honeymoon she was asked how she liked married life.

"Ah, es gefelt mir. Ich leg azey vie a princessin, er legt zich af mir, un er zapelt sich a zeh vie a mishugener."

TRANSLATION: "Ah, I like it. I lay down like a princess, and he lays on me, and then he shakes all over me like a crazy person."

The scene is a U.S. court.

The judge notices that a witness to be called next is Mr. Epstein, complete with beard, streimle and kapote. He tells his aide they'll probably need a translator for Mr. Epstein because there will probably be a language problem.

Later the bailiff calls out, "Mr. Epstein take the stand."

The judge leans over and quietly says to Mr. Epstein, "You don't have to worry, we have a Jewish interpreter."

Mr Epstein begins to speak with an English accent. "I beg your pardon, Your Honor, I am a graduate of Oxford University, majoring in English literature. I don't need an interpreter."

The interpreter chimes in, "Your Honor, er hut gezugt..."

TRANSLATION: "Your Honor, he says..."

A Yid offers the local priest an enormous amount of money if he can provide a nun to whom he could make love. It seems the Yid had slept with women in every vocation except a nun and he wanted to complete his collection.

So a deal was made and the priest sent him a nun. The Yid explains to her that she will complete his collection, and she says, "Nu, a glick hut dir getrofeen."

TRANSLATION: (Derisively) "What a stroke of luck for you."

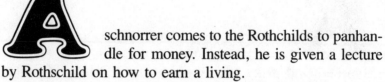 schnorrer comes to the Rothchilds to panhandle for money. Instead, he is given a lecture by Rothschild on how to earn a living.

Later, the schnorrer responds, "Vie zu machen gelt, zeit ihr a meyven. Ober, vie zu schnorren, bin ich a meyven."

TRANSLATION: "When it comes to making money, you're the expert. But, about how to schnorr, I'm the expert."

In many cultures the marriage is not truly consummated until the morning after the honeymoon night. There must be evidence that the bride was a virgin on her wedding night. And so it was in many areas in the Pale in Eastern Europe.

Anyway, this particular young couple spent the wedding night in a room that had been freshly painted green. Somehow the bed sheet became spattered with the green paint during the night.

In the morning, the mother-in-law and the witness came for the inspection. The witness commented, "In mine gantzin leben hob ich dos nit gezeyan. Mishtama hut er a zay shtark areyngeshpart az ihr gall hut avecgeplatzed."

TRANSLATION: "In my whole life I've never seen anything like this. Perhaps he must have pushed into her so hard her gall bladder must have burst."

(Medical note: Bile is stored and concentrated in the gall bladder, and is green.)

The scene is the South Bronx today. It is evening. A cop puts his hand on the shoulder of an old Jew. Sternly and firmly he says, "Come with me to the station house." The elderly Yid implores the cop, three times in Yiddish, "Why do you want me? I'm old, I've done nothing wrong."

To which the cop replies, "Ich vill nit gehn alein, ich hob meyreh."

TRANSLATION: "I don't want to go alone, I'm afraid."

A synagogue advertised for a cantor. It insisted that the applicant supply a letter of recommendation. They hired a cantor whose letter of recommendation compared him to Moses, Shakespeare and an angel.

After one week the congregation was furious. The cantor was awful. They complained to the congregation who recommended him, and also indicated that they felt they were deceived. They received an answer in reply indicating that there must have been a misunderstanding. Explaining, they said, "Er is vie Moishe Rabaynu. Moishe Rabaynu hot gehicket and der chazzan hicket. Er is vie Shakespeare. Shakespeare hut nit gekent ivre, und der chazzan ken nit kein ivre. Er is a zay vie a malech. A malech is nit a mensch, und der chazzan is ech nit kein mensch."

TRANSLATION: "He is like Moses. Moses stuttered and the cantor stutters. He is like Shakespeare. Shakespeare did not know Hebrew and the cantor does not know Hebrew. He is like an angel. An angel is not a mensch and the cantor is not a mensch."

Picture a men's room in Warsaw about 1910. Two men are standing at adjoining urinals when one feels a stream running down his right pant leg.

First man: "Well, how are things in Klodova?"

Second man: "How did you know I'm from Klodova?"

First man: "Ver is nit bekant mit die balmaluchu fun Reb Moshe der linker, der Klodover mohel?"

TRANSLATION: "Who is not acquainted with the work of Reb Moshe the Lefthanded, the Klodover mohel?" (Mohel = circumciser.)

It is Yom Kippur in the orthodox synagogue. The elders and the pious are about to prostrate themselves before the Ark.

First the rabbi extols and praises the Lord. "Oh Lord, your Torah is everlasting. It has sustained and nurtured us. And what am I, only a mortal man. I am nothing, a gornisht...ich bin a gornisht." And he prostrates himself before the Ark.

Next, he is followed by the cantor, who repeats,"Oh, Lord, your Torah is everlasting. It has sustained and nurtured us. And, what am I, only a mortal man. I am nothing, a gornisht...ich bin a gornisht." And he prostrates himself.

Suddenly, the shamus runs from the back of the synagogue to the Ark, and repeats, "Oh Lord, your Torah is everlasting. It has sustained and nurtured us. And, what am I, only a mortal man. I am nothing, a gornisht...ich bin a gornisht." And he prostrates himself before the Ark.

At that the president nudges the vice-president and says, "Gib a kuk af dem shamus, er deynkt as er iz echet a gornisht."

TRANSLATION: "Look at the shamus, he thinks he's also a nothing."

Mendel hired Feyvel, the balagolah, to transport him from Minsk to Pinsk. They started off in Feyvel's horse and wagon and soon they arrived at a steep hill.

Feyvel asked Mendel if he'd mind walking up the hill, as he doesn't think that the horse can draw the wagon and two passengers. Mendel agreed. Soon they were about to go down a hill and Feyvel asked Mendel if he wouldn't mind walking down the hill because the horse probably didn't have the strength to control the weight of the wagon and two passengers down the hill. And so, Mendel walked up the hills and down the hills to Pinsk.

When they arrived in Pinsk, Mendel asked, "Ich vill dir epis fregen. Ich hob gedarft gehen noch Pinsk, ich hob gesheft doh. Du hust gedarft gehen zu Pinsk, zu fardinen die gelt. But, zog mir, farvus hut der ferd gedarft gehen?"

TRANSLATION: "Let me ask you a question. I needed to go to Pinsk, I had business there. You needed to go to Pinsk, to earn your money. But, tell me, why did the horse have to go?"

The grandmother and grandson are strolling through the museum, past the landscapes, past the seascapes. Then, they come upon a painting of Mary in the manger.

Grandma: "Vos is dos?"

Grandson: "Der Yezel."

Grandma: "Az sie ligt in kimpet, ligt ihr in zinin tzu nemen a bild."

TRANSLATION:

"Vos is..." = "What is this?"

"Der Yezel" = "Jesus"

"Az sie..." = "Here she is in her confinement and all she's concerned about is having her portrait done."

This is a play on words. It is a real old country story where the reader must understand what it is that a tailor does.

When he sews, er nayt (he sews); when he unsews or unravels, er trent (he unsews). However, tren or trennen also means to screw or fornicate.

Anyway...

In the shetl the tailor runs to the rabbi. The tailor knows that his wife is in bed with the town milkman and he needs the rabbi to be his witness. The rabbi and the tailor go to the house. The rabbi peeks in the window and the tailor says to the rabbi, "Rebbi, git mir *an eytze*." To which the rabbi replies, "Er *neyt zie* nit, er trent zie."

TRANSLATION: (Notice *an eytze* and *neytzie*)

"Rebbi, git..." = "Rabbi, give me advice."

"Er neyt..." = "He is not sewing, he's screwing her [*or*, unravelling her]."

The young couple visited the rabbi for his advice. They were on the verge of a get (divorce). They were so unhappy. The rabbi sensed that their problem stemmed from his ineptitude and ignorance of sex. So the rabbi invited them both into the bedroom and told the young man he would show him how to make love to the young wife, and that the young man was to watch and remember everything.

Later, as the young couple was about to leave, the rabbi asked the young man, "Now, are you sure you remember everything?" At which point the wife interrupted, "Rabbi, zayt mire maychel. Veys em noch amohl. Er hot a za vershtopten kop."

TRANSLATION: "Rabbi, do me a favor. Show him once more. He is such a blockhead."

The young man is being interrogated. Unfortunately, the girl he was with has died while they were having sex.

He responded:

"Ich hob gehat mein mohl af ihr mohl,
Ein finger in ayver,
Und ein finger in toches,
Dem schmeckel in loch,
Und vie die neshomeh hut gekent arysgehen,
veys ich nit."

TRANSLATION: "I had my mouth on her mouth,
One finger in her ear,
One finger in her ass,
My penis in her hole,
And how her soul escaped from her,
I don't know."

In the shtetl, the shamus has come to fetch the rabbi for a minyan for the Holy Day. The rabbi has been standing at the marketplace watching the young women go by.

Shamus: "Nu, men darf sheyn gehen zu minyan."

Rabbi: "In harz is Tish-e-bav, ober in the hayzen is Simchas Torah."

TRANSLATION: "Nu, men..." = "We need to go to the prayers."

"In harz..." = "In my heart it's Tishe [any unhappy holiday], but in my pants it's Simchas Torah [a happy holiday]."

Two Jews meet on a street one day.

The first: "Hymie, du kenst Abie mitten hayker?"

The second: "Abie mitten hayker? Ich ken em nit."

The first: "Du kenst Abie? Er hut a loch in kop."

The second: "A loch in kop? Ich ken em nit."

The first: "Ich vell dir geben a simen. Er hut a fakrimpter noz."

The second: "A loch in kop, un a fakrimpter noz? Ich ken em nit."

The first: "Ich vell dir geben noch a simen. Er hut a loch in kop, und a ferkrimpter noz, und ret fun seit fuhn mohl."

The second: "Ich ken em nit."

The first: "Ich vell dir geben noch a simen. Er hut a loch in kop und a ferikrimpter noz, a tzedreyter mohl, und er hot a hayker."

The second: "Ich ken em nit."

The first: "Ich vell dir geben noch a simen. Er hust a loch in kopf, und a ferkrimpter noz, a tzedreyter mohl, und er hot a hayker, un er schlept a fuss."

The second: "Oh, dos Abie, em ken ich ganz gut. Vos is die mehr?"

The first: "Er is avec geshtorben."

The second: "Oy, a za shaynem Yid."

TRANSLATION: The first: "Hymie, do you know Abie, with the hunched back?"

The second: "Abie the hunchback? No, I don't know him."

The first: "Don't you know Abie? He's got a hole in his head."

The second: "A hole in his head? No, I don't know him."

The first: "I'll give you another clue. He's got a crooked nose."

The second: "A hole in his head and a crooked nose? No, I don't know him."

The first: "Well, I'll give you another clue. He's got a hole in his head, and a crooked nose, and he talks through the side of his mouth."

The second" "No, I don't know him."

The first: "I'll give you another clue. He's got a hole in his head, and a crooked nose, and he talks through the side of his mouth, and he has a hunchback."

The second: "No, I don't know him."

The first: "I'll give you another clue. He's got a hole in his head, and a crooked nose, and he talks through the side of his mouth, and he's got a hunchback, and he drags his leg."

The second: "Oh, that Abie. I know him very well. What's the matter?"

The first: "He died."

The second: "Oh, he was such a beautiful man."

A Jewish woman goes to her doctor to complain about an embarrassing problem. She explains that she breaks wind without any smell or odor and it's most embarrassing.

So he asks her to step on a ladder so he can get an eye-level demonstration, and she does. After which the doctor says, "Mir muz opereran."

"Du geyst opereran offen toches?"

"Nein, aafen noz!"

TRANSLATION: "Mir muz..." = "We'll have to operate."
"Du geyst..." = "You're going to operate on my ass?"
"Nein, affen..." = "No, on your nose!"

Lapidus is a manufacturer of shmatas on 7th Avenue—vary haute couture. The shop is having their pre-vacation party and at least 15 of the most beautiful models in New York are there. He looks around and observes that he had tried to go to bed with at least five, but had always been impotent and unable to perform.

He goes home and observes his wife washing the kitchen floor. Her hair is a mess, she wears a kitchen dress at least four sizes too big, and he begins to feel a stirring in him and he develops an erection.

He mutters to himself as he glances down at his penis, "Yetzt veys ich farvos men ruhft dir a putz."

TRANSLATION: "Now I know why they call you a putz."

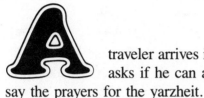 traveler arrives in town, goes to the rabbi and asks if he can assemble a minyan so he can say the prayers for the yarzheit.

With effort they assemble nine. The rabbi tells his wife to go out and ask the first man she meets to come to make the tenth man.

It is raining, and she is a mess. She sees a man and asks, "Du vilst zein dem tzenta?"

To which he replied, "Nit dem eshter afileh."

TRANSLATION: "Du vilst..." = "Do you want to be the tenth?"

"Nit dem..." = "I wouldn't even want to be the first."

Picture the kitchen of a small home in the shtetl.
She comes home and finds her husband soaking his genitals for relief in a bowl, and yells at him, "Nem aroys die fleish fuhn dem milchidicken tup."

TRANSLATION: "Take the meat out of the dairy pot."

The scene is Miami Beach. Two widows are together. The first woman, observing the weather, says, "Es schmekt regen."

The second woman replies, "Alivey, vet regen schmeck."

TRANSLATION: (Note: Schmekt equals smell; schmeck equals the plural of schmuck, or more than one penis. Therefore...)

"Es schmekt..." = "It smells like rain."

"Alivey, vet..." = "Hopefully, it will rain penises."

The 75-year-old husband awoke his wife with the grand announcement: "Es shteht."

She is elated, but announced she'll be right back, "Ich muz gayn pishin."

It took her quite awhile and when she returned he said, "Verlossen, du kenst gayn kacken echet."

TRANSLATION: "Es shtayt" = "I have an erection."
"Ich muz..." = "I have to take a pee."
"Verlossen, du..." = "All is lost, you can also take a crap for yourself."

The bubbie is teaching the grandaughter how to cook.

By accident an egg falls on the floor. "Nu, ich vell shayn machen a kugel."

TRANSLATION: "Well, I may as well make a pudding."

housewife visits her local butcher, and prices a cut of chuck.

"Lady, this chuck weighs six pounds and costs $2.60 a pound."

The customer leaves without making a purchase. However a half hour later she returns and asks the price again, and leaves, and returns again in a half hour to ask the butcher the price yet again.

In annoyance he says, "Chuck isn't shmuck. Es shteht nit and es falt nit, und es is nuch $2.60 a funt."

TRANSLATION: "Chuck is not a penis. It does not rise and fall and it still costs $2.60 a pound."

A choir advertised for a basso singer.

Our hero responded. When he asked if they had advertised for a basso they noted that his voice was high pitched, almost falsetto.

So, he was not accepted for the job. When he asked why, he was told, "Eyer stimme is not grub genug."

Our hero in his falsetto voice, responded, "Nu kush mir in toches, dos is grub genug?

TRANSLATION: (Note: Grub can mean deep and can also mean coarse or crude.)

"Eyer stimme..." = "Your voice is not deep enough."

"Nu, kush mir..." = "So, kiss my ass, is that crude enough?"

Mr. Epstein had been waiting for his train, and while waiting he amuses himself at the scale. Every time he puts in a penny, out comes a card giving his weight and a witticism or wise saying.

Finally, he gets a card that reads, "Schmuck, du bist noch doh? Dein bahn hart farlossen mit finif minuten zurick.

TRANSLATION: "You schmuck, are you still here? You're train left five minutes ago."

An impotent man goes to the rabbi for advice. The rabbi recommends that he put his penis in the torah, saying, "Alles shteht in torah."

TRANSLATION: "Everything 'stands' in the torah."

The bride has returned from her honeymoon. The tanta wants to know, "Nu, how did it go?"

"Mir hoben gegangen tzu bet, hot er mir gevorfen affen bet, un areyn geshtupt a stick fleish voh ich pish. A glick hot mir getroffen! Abe er vot mir getroffen en eig, vot ich govorin blynd."

TRANSLATION: "We went to bed. He threw me on the bed, put a piece of meat where I pee. Was I lucky! If he had gotten me in the eye, I would be blind."

Our hero saw an ad in the newspaper. A safari group was being assembled and the ad stated they were looking for a man with the eye of an eagle, the heart of a lion, the strength of a bull.

Our hero, a Yeshiva student—frail, double-thick glasses, weak-looking, thin—responded, "Did you advertise for someone with the eye of an eagle, the heart of a lion, the strength of a bull? Ich vill eich sogin, as af mir solst du sich nit verlossen."

TRANSLATION: "I want to tell you, that you shouldn't depend on me."

The scene is the mikvah (indoor bath or pool) in the shtetl. There is pandemonium and disorder. The rebetzen is trying to force her way to the head of the line.

And to each person ahead she would say, "Anshuldig, ich bin die rebetzen, the rebbe vart far mir."

Finally the last lady ahead replies, "Nu, los em varten, ich bin die kurveh, un de gantze shtetl vart far mir."

TRANSLATION: "Anshuldig..." = "Excuse me, I'm the rabbi's wife, and the rabbi is waiting for me."
"Nu los..." = "So, let him wait, I'm the town whore, and the whole town is waiting for me."

The scene is a room in the local brothel.

The client asks why she keeps a candle lit in the corner. He'd prefer to be in the dark.

She explains she can't turn out the light since, "Ich hob yahrzeit for die bubbie."

TRANSLATION: "I have yahrzeit for my grandmother."

The aging father was finally admitted to a home for the elderly. It was a very posh institution with a high level of care.

One day the children came to visit the father and decided to observe him from a doorway before they entered his room.

The father was sitting in a chair with an aide on the left, and an aide on the right. Periodically, the father would lean to the left, and the aide would straighten him up, then he'd lean to the right, and the aide would straighten him up.

Finally the children entered and asked the father how things were going. He answered, "Alles is gut, ober ein zach, ven ich vill geben a fortz, men lost nit."

TRANSLATION: "Everything is good, but for one thing, when I want to fart, they won't let me."

An American couple wanted to fulfill a life-long ambition to visit Paris in the springtime. They booked a flight for mid-May and in the meantime went to night school to study conversational French.

Finally, in the springtime they arrived in Paris. It is early evening when they hail a taxi and instruct the driver to take them to a restaurant in the suburbs and to make sure they will be with only Frenchmen, absolutely no tourists. They arrive at a neighborhood restaurant and are seated in the midst of people having lively conversations. At the next table they hear the following conversation:

"Figurez vous la chutzpah de cette goy. Shabbos, le matin, quand je suis revenu de la shul, on me donne un cafe kalt. Quelle shlamazel."

TRANSLATION: "Can you figure the audacity of the gentile? Saturday morning, when I was returning from the synagogue, someone gave me a cold cup of coffee. What bad luck."

urphy Shapiro's Law:
"Az es geht ken men schissen mit a bezem."

TRANSLATION: "When you're lucky, when things are going your way, you can shoot with a broom."

The mother had tried very hard to find a suitor for the daughter, but every time the schadchen brought a young man, he was chased away by the remarks of the outspoken, vulgar, coarse, aggressive father. The mother and schadchen finally convinced the father that his only chance to have a married daughter was to keep his mouth shut, and to speak only in response to a question.

The following week a young man is brought to the house for lunch. The mother notices that the father is not eating the chicken soup. (She doesn't realize that he doesn't have a spoon.)

She: "Farvoss est du nit deyn soup?"

He: "Mit voss zohl ich essen, mine putz?"

TRANSLATION: She: "Why aren't you eating your soup?"

He: "What shall I use to eat it with, my putz [my penis]?"

Cohen was emotionally overwhelmed during the 1967 United Jewish Appeal Drive. He pledges a contribution of $10,000. He never paid the pledge nor did he make another contribution. Finally, in 1970 he was sued and had to pay the pledge plus court costs.

Again in 1973 he attended a fund raising meeting. The speaker made an impassioned plea for funds, and asked, "Who will be the first person to pledge $10,000. Up jumped Cohen declaring, "I'll pledge $10,000 plus court costs!"

The "greenhorn" is reporting on the first time she went to the theater.

"Ven sie vill, vil er nit,
Ven er vill, vill sie nit,
Ven zeh beyde villen, hoben zay vermacht der verhang."

TRANSLATION: "When she wanted to, he didn't.
When he wanted to, she didn't
When they both wanted to, down came the curtain."

Everyone wanted to know how Rabbi Sean Ferge-son got his name, because they knew he came from Poland. He explained, "Meine cousina hut mir gesogt az zey vellen mir fregan vos is mine nomen zoll ich zogen John Smith, ober ven der inspector hut mir gefregt hub ich geentfert az ich hob sheyn fergessen."

TRANSLATION: "My cousin told me to say my name was John Smith when the inspector would ask, but I told him I forgot [Ich hob sheyn fergessen]."

The mother goes to see the schadchen for her daughter.

The schadchen says:

"Ich ken ihr,   (I know her)

A sheine is sie nit,   (She's no beauty)

A kluge is sie nit   (She's not too smart)

Ober, sog mir, is sie a heise?"   (But tell me is she hot?)

(Note: Heise could mean hot in temperature or passionately hot.)

The mother says, "Ich vell ihr fregen." (I'll ask her.)

So she goes home, and repeats the conversation to her daughter, "Er ken dir, ehr veyst az du bist nit a sheine, ehr veys az du bist nit a kluge, ober ehr vill vissen ob du bist a heise?" (He wants to know if you're hot?)

Daughter: "Ich veys nit, ober ven ich pish geht fun mir a pareh."

TRANSLATION: "I don't know, but when I piss, a storm of steam blows up."

An elderly Jewish woman visits the gynecologist for the first time. After the examination, she asks the doctor, "Deyn momma veyst vie du mochst a leben?"

TRANSLATION: "Does your mother know what you do to earn a living?"

The scene is the Lower East Side about 1910. He's pushing his pushcart, loaded with coal which he sells in 50-pound bags. On Houston Street he hollers his wares, "Kaylen—kaylen" (Coal—coal).

He spots a lady on the fourth floor of a tenement, she motions and waves one finger, indicating she wants one bag of coal.

He trudges up, carrying the 50-pound bag. When he gets to her apartment, she explains that she has no money, but she'll go to bed with him for payment.

He answers, "Sheyne veibele, ich kennit, ich hob shon oisgetrent 200 funt kayen keint."

TRANSLATION: "Pretty lady, I can't. I've already screwed away 200 pounds of coal today."

This must be the quintessential Jewish guilt story.
His mother bought him two ties for his birthday gift. The next day he is wearing one when he visits his mother. She: "Vos is, der anderer gefelt dir nit?"

TRANSLATION: "What's the matter, didn't like the other one?"

The man went to see his well-to-do rabbi, to seek clarification of a question.

Is sex work or pleasure?

Rabbi: "Mishtomeh is dos a fargeniggen, a nit vot mein veib gemacht die deinst es tuhn."

TRANSLATION: "It's probably a pleasure, otherwise my wife would have the maid do it."

An old, old country lady is watching the movie *Ben Hur.* Suddenly she hollers, "Halten der film!" The usher comes over and asks what the problem is and why is she making such a ruckus.

She: "The lions are eating the Jews."

He: "But lady they are eating the Christians, not Jews."

That seemed to quiet and comfort her, so the film resumes, but five minutes later she begins to holler again, "Halten der film."

"Usher: "Vos is?"

She: "Der layb in vinkle est nit."

TRANSLATION: "That lion in the corner is not eating."

This is an old country story.

       Two partners had a practice of dividing every-thing. One day they found an egg. They discussed how to divide the egg, but reached an impasse, so they went to see the rabbi for his advice.

After some contemplation the rabbi said, "Ein schmuck mit tsvei eyer hob is gesehen. Ober tsvei schmeck mit ein ey hob ich kein mohl nit gesehen."

TRANSLATION: "I've seen one penis with two testicles, but I've never seen two schmucks [actually the plural is schmeck] with one egg."

    Note: Schmuck can mean 1) penis or 2) a foolish person. Eyer (plural of ey) can mean 1) eggs or 2) testicles.

Two Jews go to China. They stay in a hotel where the walls are paper thin. Early in the morning, number one wakes number two and says, "Kum shayn Shimshon, Shimshon kum shayn." (Come, wake up Shimson. Shimson, wake up.)

The Chinese spy on the other side of the wall says, "Boy those Jews are marvelous. One day in China, and they speak Chinese already."

A rabbi and a bus driver stand before the divine court. The driver is assigned to heaven and the rabbi is not. The rabbi protests and he argues that he was pious, clean, observant, reverent, and gentle, whereas the bus driver was coarse, a non-believer and a non-observer. The registrar says, "Rebbe, ven du host gegeben a drosha hoben alle geshloffen, ober ven er hut getribben, hoben alle gedavent."

TRANSLATION: "Rabbi, when you gave a sermon everyone slept, when he drove everyone prayed."

The son is about to get married and is asking his father for advice on how to behave on his wedding night.

The father advises, "Nahm the greste zach vos du host, and leg es aryen vu zie pisht."

TRANSLATION: "Take the biggest thing you've got and put it where she pees."

So on his wedding night he took his shoe and threw it into the toilet.

Two men are walking down the street.

Number one says: "Did you hear about the two old Jews?"

Number two says: "Look I'm sick and tired of hearing about two old Jews, always the old Jews. Can't you change it over to someone else?"

Number one says: "Ok, these two old Italians were walking down the street, and one says, 'Nu, Beryl, vu gehst du avec far Pesach?'"

TRANSLATION: "Well, Beryl, where are you going away for Passover?"

There is an old wive's tale that the best time of the year to die is on Rosh Chodesh Nissan (the first day of the Hebrew lunar month of Nissan). Some old women believe that on this day, which is two weeks before Passover, the angels are too busy checking up on the preparations for Passover, and so it's easy to slip into heaven.

In the neighborhood on Rosh Chodesh Nissan sat some of the older country Jewish women. A hearse passes by.

Lady number one: "Ver hot gestorben?" (Who died?)

Lady number two: "Mrs. Spellacy."

Lady number one: "Oy, the goyim hoben alle mazel!"

TRANSLATION: "The gentiles have all the luck."

He was a famous actor on the Yiddish stage. His King Lear was the standard by which others were judged. But he was a womanizer too. One afternoon he picked up a hip young girl and took her back to the hotel for sex. As she was about to leave he gave her two tickets for the evening performance of his show.

She: "Billeten darf ich nit. Ich darf breit. Ich bin a nafkeh."

He: "Breit villst du mein kind, as azeh nexten mohl zolst du sich avec legen trennen mit a becker."

TRANSLATION: She: "Tickets I don't need. I need bread. I'm a prostitute."

He: "So next time if you want bread screw a baker."

She was married for a long time but couldn't conceive. She finally decided to visit the rabbi, after none of the doctors were able to help her. The rabbi pondered her problem for a while and finally pronounced very sagely his advice if she wanted a child. "Keyf a bagel." (Buy a bagel.)

Five months later the rabbi meets her on the street and she's visibly pregnant. She tells the rabbi how smart he is, how brilliant to tell her to buy a bagel when he did.

She: "Ich hob gegeben the lechem zum man, and dem loch zum boarder."

TRANSLATION: "I gave the bread to my husband and the hole to the boarder."

very heavy lady tells the doctor about the enormous amounts of food she eats. She doesn't feel well and wants his advice.

She: "Nu, Doktor, vos darf ich?"

Dr.: "Ihr darft hoben noch a loch in toches."

TRANSLATION: She "Well, Doctor, what do I need?"

Dr.: "You need another hole in your ass."

The cantor told the synagogue committee that he would have to leave his job, he just was not earning enough money. They pleaded with him to wait one more day before he made a final decision. They would try to solve the problem.

The next day they met again. "Please don't go, we can't give you more money but listen to what we can do."

The butcher said that he would give him meat at no charge three times a week.

The baker promised him bread at no charge five times a week.

The garage man promised him ten gallons of gas a week.

The sisterhood president stood up, "Ich vill eich trennen zwei mohl a voch, yeden Montag and Mitwoch." (Translation: "I will screw you two times a week, Monday and Wednesday.")

A hush fell over the room, finally someone asked her why she said what she did.

She said, "Ich hob gefregt mine man vos ken ich geben dem chazen, hut er gesogt, 'Fuck him.'"

TRANSLATION: "I asked my husband what I could give the cantor, he said, 'Fuck him.'"

ritzy Jewish lady is walking and observes an old Jew urinating on the side of a building.

She: (Contemptuously) "A zay grub."

He: (With a sense of elegance and pride) "Un lang, echet."

TRANSLATION: (Grub is a word that has several meanings. It can mean thick, coarse, boorish, or vulgar.)

She: "You are vulgar."

He: "And long, too."

Two 80-year-olds are in their rockers. One begins to leave, he tries to push himself out of the chair, he slips, he grunts, he groans, he strains, and finally pushes himself out of the rocker, and begins to shuffle along.

His friend says, "Beryl, vu leyfst du?"

TRANSLATION: "Where are you running?"

The Yiddish teacher asks the students to give examples of how the phrase "efsher a mohl" could be used. (Translation of "efsher a mohl" is "perhaps, under certain circumstances.")

Student number one: "Efsher a mohl keyft men burikes macht men borsh.." (Translation—"Sometime if you buy beets you can make borscht [beet soup]."

Student number two: "Efsher a mohl keyft men kartoffel, macht men latkes." (Translation—"Sometime you can buy potatoes, and you can make potato pancakes.")

Student number three: "Ich hob areyn gekukt duch a loch in vant und gesehen vie mine schwester nemt arop ihre heisen, und ihr lehrer hut arop seine heisen, efsher a mohl gehen zey onpishen afen pianeh."

TRANSLATION: "I looked through a hole in the wall, and saw my sister take off her pants, and her teacher removed his pants, perhaps they would both piss on the piano."

crowd has gathered around the body of a man who has fallen to the ground. The mood is hushed.

Upon the scene comes an old country "greener Yid" and says, "Gib em a kaneh." (Give him an enema.)

A bystander explains. "He's dead. We've tried mouth-to-mouth. We've tried CPR."

The Yid says, "Es kennit shotten."

TRANSLATION: "It couldn't hurt."

A man had a wife who was an incessant talker; it seemed that she never stopped. The husband went with her to visit the doctor for an ailment, and he noticed that the only time she was quiet was when the doctor put the thermometer in her mouth.

The husband asked, "Doctor, dem mashinkeh, vos kost es?"

TRANSLATION: "Doctor, that little machine, how much does it cost."

This is the story of the nine-year-old, who bet his friend that he could get his grandfather to imitate an owl.

The boy: "Zayde, gib a kuk, af die shayne maydel."

Grandpa: "Voo, VOO."

TRANSLATION: The Boy: "Zayde, look at the beautiful girl."

Grandpa: "Where, *where*?"

A woman threatened her husband:
"When I die, I don't want you to remarry, because if you do I'll dig myself out and haunt you." Later when she died he arranged to have her buried with her face down. Then he went to her grave and said, "Grub, grub."

TRANSLATION: "Dig, dig."

pious Yid is seen as he is about to walk into a bawdy house, and he's wearing his talis (prayer shawl).

An acquaintance says: "Reb Yid, varvus geit ihe in shandeh hois mitten Talis."

"Eb is gefelt mir, vell ich bleiben uber die yomteyvim."

TRANSLATION: "Learned Sir, why are you going into a brothel wearing your prayer shawl?"
"If this place pleases me, I'll stay over the holidays."

The scene is a kosher butcher shop. The butcher notices that the customer has a chicken in her hand one minute, the next minute she turns around, and then turns again and the chicken has disappeared. She obviously has stolen the chicken and hidden it on her person.

So, he sticks his hand into her dress over her left tit, and astonishedly he declares, "Oy gevald, azeh shnell shein opgeflicked."

TRANSLATION: "So fast, the chicken is plucked clean."
(Note, in a kosher meat market—the old-fashioned kind, before freezers—one would buy a live chicken and later have it dressed.)

The scene is the same hotel room the couple had gone to on their honeymoon 50 years ago. He asks his darling if she remembers that on their honeymoon, she didn't even give him a chance to take his stockings off.

She remembered.

"Nu, heint banacht kenst du mir stricken a por zocken."

TRANSLATION: "Well, tonight you can knit a pair of socks for me."

This is the story of a teacher in the cheyder (a religious school) and the hell raiser, the "bad boy." Oh, he was a wild one. One day the teacher had to put him in the corner for misbehaving.

At ten o'clock the boy asked how long he would have to stand in the corner, and the teacher said he would let him know. The same question and answer at 11 o'clock and at 12 and one. At one o'clock the kid said he would like to eat, "I'm hungry. I want to eat, how long do I have to stand here." The teacher told him till three.

The boy said, "Biz drei, kenst mir kushen in toches drei azeyger." (At three you can kiss my ass.) With that the teacher decided to answer that insolence with a thrashing, but by the time the teacher got his stick the youngster jumped out of the window and started to run away. The teacher started to run after him and after a few minutes he was exhausted and he met a friend who asked,

"Vu leyfst du?"

"Ich leyf noch dem yingle, zu mir hut er gesogt az ich ken em kushin in tochas drei azeyger."

"Nu, vos yugst du, es is not einse azeiger."

TRANSLATION: "Vu leyfst..." = "Where are you running to, what's your hurry?"

"Ich leyf..." = "I'm running after that boy, he told me to kiss his ass at three o'clock."

"Well, what's your hurry, it's only one o'clock."

89

Jake bought fabric in Italy to make a new suit. He took the fabric to five different tailors and all told him he didn't have enough fabric to make a suit.

Finally he went to Lapidus the tailor, who said that he could make a suit, that there was plenty of cloth.

When Jake went to pick up the suit, which incidentally fit him perfectly, the tailor's son walked in wearing a suit of the same cloth.

Jake was amazed, and asked how he had enough fabric, when the other tailors said they didn't.

Lapidus: "Vielicht, zeinen the andere yingelich gresser."

TRANSLATION: "Maybe the sons of the other tailors were bigger."

The Benevolent Society was meeting for their annual election, and the fight for the chairman's seat was hotly contested by Levy and Cohen.

Levy's campaign manager was beginning the nominating speech and said he would describe his candidate through the letters of the alphabet.

"A he is ambitious
B he is benevolent
C he is clever
D he is damn clever
E he is efficient
F he is friendly
G he is generous
H he is honest
I he is intelligent
J he is judicious"

At that point Cohen's manager said that he had to interrupt and would finish the list of qualities, and without waiting, continued,

K er is a kacker   (a shitter)
L er is a loiz   (a louse)
M er is a momzer   (a bastard)
N er is a nudnik   (a terrible pest)
O er is a oisvurf   (an outcast)
P er is a pisher   (a pee-er) meaning wet behind the ears,
                           unseasoned.

Q er is a quevetch   (a complainer)
R er is a rat   (a rat)
S er is a stinker   (a stinker)
T er is a trombenick (a scoundrel)
U er is a unick   (eunuch)
V er is a vantz   (a bedbug)
and WXYZ er is an
S.O.B.

This is the story of the elderly lady who is going by train from New York to Washington to visit her older daughter. The youngest daughter takes the mother to the train station, she helps her get a seat, puts her baggage on the upper rack, and leaves a zippered bag with food on the next seat. Everything is under control, and Momma is left on the train. Soon she begins to doze and falls asleep. Around Philadelphia a young man needs a seat and puts her bag of food on the rack and sits next to her. About a half hour later the elderly lady begins to stir, and as she is half awake, reaches over and opens the zipper (she doesn't realize it's the zipper of the man's pants and not of the food bag), and she puts her hand inside.

"Ay is dos a guten tochter, der helzel is noch varm."

TRANSLATION: "Oh, my daughter is wonderful. [How well she packaged.] The neck [of the chicken] is still warm."

Lapidus ate his lunch in the same restaurant every day for twelve years, and every day he sat at the same table and had the same waiter.

The waiter noticed that no matter what Lapidus ordered, whether fish, steak, or salad, he would begin by cutting a slice of whatever he was eating and place it in his vest pocket.

After twelve years the waiter could no longer contain his curiosity and asked about the procedure, why did he cut the first piece and put it in his pocket?

"Ich vays az nine partner vill az ich vel dershticken offen ershten beis,"

TRANSLATION: "I know that my partner hopes that I'll choke on my first bite."

This is a story which takes place about 1910, when it cost $24 to cross the Atlantic by boat in steerage. The accommodations for sleeping are awful, sometimes the bunk beds are stacked five high. On this particular journey two friends are traveling together and their sleeping set-up is one bunk over the other. In the middle of the night the man in the upper bunk has to answer a nature call, and he reaches down trying to locate his chamber pot, but instead grabs hold of his friend's penis.

The man on the lower bunk hollers up,

"Vos tust du, vos vilst du?"

"Ich darf oispishen."

"Mit vos, mit mine putz?"

TRANSLATION: "Vos tust..." = "What are you doing, what do you want?"

"Ich darf..." = I need to pee."

"Mit vos..." = "With what, with my putz [penis]?"

In the shtetl two men decide to settle a dispute. When they arrive at the rabbi's home, they discover that he's not at home, but the rabbi's wife suggests that perhaps she can be of some help in settling the dispute. After all, she's been married for 25 years and has been the rabbi's confidant.

The two men agree to have her settle their dispute. Number one says that man number two is the world's greatest "ochshen" (a very stubborn person who can't be moved from his position), and number two says that number one is.

The rebetzen tells them their both wrong. She is the greatest ochshen. She remembers that 25 years ago she and the rabbi got married, and when they went on their honeymoon, they found twin beds. He wouldn't come to her bed, and she wouldn't go to his bed.

When they returned home they slept in twin beds. Ever since, he wouldn't come to her bed, and she wouldn't go to his bed.

Finally, number one says, "Rebetzen, vos redst du a nareshhkeit, du host five kinder."

"Kinder takeh hob ich. Nor Shmeryl, der shamus, is nit kein ochshen."

TRANSLATION: Number one: "Why are you talking so foolishly, you have five children."

"I do have five children, but Shmeryl, the sexton, is not a stubborn man."

A n older Jewish lady goes to the travel agent and wants to book a flight to Katmandu, Nepal.

The travel agent tries to dissuade her. He explains that it is a rigorous trip and the country is very primitive. She threatens, "Book me, or I'll go to another agent."

In Katmandu, she goes to another travel agent to arrange a trip to a certain monastery. He explains to her that it is a three-day journey, up the mountains, down the mountains, it's cold, and windy and primitive. She threatens, "Book me, or I'll go to another agent."

After an arduous journey she finally arrives at the monastery and insists on seeing the guru. At first the monks refuse, but when they perceive her resolve they finally agree that she can see the guru on the following Friday, but only for three minutes and she can only say three words. She agrees.

On Friday she is brought into his presence. The room is dark, he is seated in the lotus position. He bows slightly from the waist. The woman begins to breathe deeply, and heavily, she points to the guru and shouts, "Kum nit aheim!"

TRANSLATION: "Don't come home!"

Three old Jews are complaining to each other about their ailments.

Old man number one: "Look at me, look at my tsoreh (my affliciton). I need to wear these thick glasses in order to read."

Old man number two: "Look at me. My tsoreh is that I need to wear this hearing aid or I can't hear anything."

Old man number three: "My friends, my problem is by far the most serious. Last night I tried to wake my wife at two a.m. with the announcement: 'Es shteht.' (Translation: 'I have an erection.') But what did my wife do? She got angry, told me that I was crazy and that we had been together only a half hour earlier. "Ah, meine friender, dosh is mine tsoreh. Ich gedeynk gornit."

TRANSLATION: "Ah, my friends, that's my affliction. I don't remember anything."

Old Mr. Cohen finally was at the gates of heaven; however, the registrar told him that there were problems. The registrar wasn't sure he could admit him. Mr. Cohen had been so pious on earth and had never committed a transgression, but even the purest of angels had some kind of blemish, and no one could be admitted who was purer than the angels.

Perhaps Mr. Cohen could be returned to earth for one day, and commit some little transgression. Then he could be admitted at once to heaven.

So Mr. Cohen returns to the old neighbrhood and Mrs. Lapidus spots him and invites him in for tea. Then she confesses that she always admired him, and respected him and since she was a widow would consider it a great honor to go to bed with Mr. Cohen if he was interested.

Aha! He thinks to himself, this will be my transgression, my passport to heaven.

Into bed they go. Then later as he's dressing and almost ready to return to heaven, Mrs. Lapidus turns to him, sweetly, and says, "Du bist a zah sheyer mensch, du host vardient a mitzvah."

TRANSLATION: "You are such a good man, what you did is a mitzvah [good deed]." (Certainly not a transgression.)

This is the story about the father and daughter riding in the horse and wagon in the countryside. Suddenly, two bandits overtake them and take away the horse and wagon.

They are downcast. But while walking, the daughter tells the father that the jewelry she had is safe. It was hidden between her legs.

The father resonds, "Ob die mamma is doh gevesen, vot sie behalten dem ferd und vogen, echet."

TRANSLATION: "If your mother was here, she could have hidden the horse and wagon, too."

The rabbi visits the mikvah (ritual bath) and he keeps repeating the count, 15–16–17. He tells his assistant that he doesn't understand why he can't reconcile the count. There are nine women and he should count 18 tits, and he only counts to 17.

The assistant says, "Rebbe, ein tzitzke halt ihr in hant."

TRANSLATION: "Rabbi, you're holding one tit in your hand."

 woman of sharp tongue who is abusive and generally nasty goes to see the rabbi and explains that she's thinking about taking the boat to America and she wants his reaction.

The rabbi says: "Gold sheint in bluteh ober drek schwint off wasser."

TRANSLATION: "Gold shines in the mud [dirt] but shit floats on water."

The anthropologist is down on the Lower East Side. He's fascinated with some of the characteristics of Jewish family life in the 1920's, particularly the close, warm, gentle relationships between grandparents and grandchildren. How do the words of wisdom flow from one generation to another? The anthropologist walks past a grandfather talking to his grandson and hears the grandfather, who has a long white beard, admonishing his five-year-old grandson, "Vifel mohl darf ich dir sogon az zu an alter zeyde sogt min nit fok you?"

TRANSLATION: "How many times have I told you, that to an old grandfather you don't say fuck you?"

The vilest man in town had died. The local rabbi refused to officiate at the funeral. He said that he wouldn't be able to say a single complimentary word.

So the family tried the next town, and the next, and finally they found a rabbi who didn't know the deceased and who was willing to officiate at the funeral.

At the eulogy he begins to extol the great virtues of the deceased—his kindness, his philanthropies, his good deeds.

The mother nudges the oldest son. "Gey, gib a kuk in crooneh un zeh verh ligt dorten?"

TRANSLATION: "Look in the coffin, and see who is in there."

The older women are talking about the "monkey gland operation."

Woman number one: "Since Jake had the 'monkey gland operation' it's like being a bride again. He doesn't go to sleep right away in bed, and he's an active young man again."

Sorkeh comes home and tells her husband, Moishe, about the operation. She pesters him to get the operation, so he goes to the surgeon. The surgeon tells him that the operation costs $10,000. Moishe says it's too much money, anything cheaper? The doctor explains that they're experimenting on dog glands. The results are not in yet, but that operation costs only $1,500.

"Ok, I'll do it."

About a month later, Sorkeh is asked about how things are going since the operation. "Nu, er lekt a bissel, ehr shmekt a bissel, den pisht er zich ois offen vant!"

TRANSLATION: "Now he licks a little, he sniffs a little and then he pees on the wall!"

golfer tells his wife that he hears all the young, modern men talking in the locker room, bragging about how their wives groan during sex, and how wonderful it is.

He: "Do you think you can groan?"

She: "Yes, but tell me when. I think I can do it."

So when they're making love, she asks, "Now?" He replies, "No, not yet."

A little bit later she asks again. "Now?" He replies, "No, not yet."

A few minutes later she asks again, "Now?" He replies, "Yes, now!"

She shouts out: "Oy, heint is gevesen a zah bekackten tog!"

TRANSLATION: "Oy, today was such a shitty day!"

The story about the son who discovers his father at the "shandeh hois" (the brothel).

Son: "Tata, vos tust du doh?'

Father: "Fahr 50¢ leynt sich nit zu nudgenen die mama."

TRANSLATION: "What are you doing here?"
"For 50¢ it's not worth it to bother your mother."

The mother visits the schadchen. She wants a husband for her daughter.

A prospective son-in-law is found, but he insists on seeing the prospective bride in the nude before he can make a final decision.

The family agrees to this unconventional request. After half an hour in the room with the girl he comes out and declares that he will not marry her.

"Sie gefelt mir nit. Sie hut a krumer noz."

TRANSLATION: "She doesn't satisfy me. She has a crooked nose."

Two women are talking:

Lady number one: "Lately Jake has been very romantic. Last Sunday he bought me flowers, and all week I've been on my back, with my legs in the air."

Lady number two: "Vos is, du hust nit a vazeh?"

TRANSLATION: "Don't you have a vase?"

Three friends are sitting together in the shtetl. The three are Beryl, Peryl, and Shmeryl. They are talking about their dreams, about the time they will be able to go to America.

Beryl explains that one of the first things he'll do when he goes to America to become Americanized will be to take a Yankee name. He's decided he will change his name from Beryl to Buck.

Peryl thinks that's a good idea, and he's going to change his name from Peryl to Puck.

Shmeryl ponders a moment and says, "Ich for nit kin America."

TRANSLATION: "I'm not going to America,"

GLOSSARY

GLOSSARY

Avera = a transgression.

Balagolah = a teamster; one who drives a horse and wagon.

Bubbie = a grandmother.

Cantor = a professional vocalist who assists at synagogue services; also known as a chazzen.

Eydele meydel = a refined, gentle, unmarried girl.

Gabeh = an honorary officer of a synagogue.

Gornisht = a nobody; a person of no worth in the community, or thinks of himself as having no worth as a person.

Goy = anyone who is not Jewish.

Kapote = a long formal black coat, normally worn with a fur hat (streimle).

Kurveh = a prostitute; whore.

Lag Baomer = a Jewish festival day; "the thirty-third day of the Omer."

Litvack = a Yid from Litte or Lithuania.

Mensch = a man who has good character and a strong sense of responsibility.

Meyse = a story.

Minyan = in order to pray as a congregation, ten Jews over 13 years of age must be present; in some congregations only males may be included in the ten, in some congregations women as well as men are counted.

Mitzvah = "Dear Abby" defines it as "an act to help his fellow man"; there are 613 mitzvos.

Pale of Settlement = In Czarist Russia, starting in 1791, 95% of the Jews could only live in an area of about 4% of Russian land known as a Pale.

Mohel = a Jewish, ritual circumciser.

Putz = slang for penis; generally used to describe someone off small brain power or poor judgement.

Rebetzen = the wife of a rabbi.

Schadchen = an introducer or matchmaker who collects a fee if a marriage results from the introduction arranged.

Shamus = the sexton of a synagogue.

Shmata = a rag; however, in the parlance of 7th Avenue, it is the product manufactured in a dress factory.

Shul = a synagogue.

Schlamazel = an unlucky person; the classic example: if a waiter stumbles and pours the soup on your head he is the shlemiel but you are the schlamazel.

Schnorrer = a professional Jewish beggar.

Shtetl = the small towns in Czarist Russia where 95% of the Jews were confined in the Pale of Settlement, and where they were insulated from the general, larger society.

Streimle = the black fur hat normally worn by Hassidim.

Tanta = an aunt.

Yarzheit = the anniversary of the date of death.

Yeshiva = in Europe, a place for advanced study of Torah and Talmud.